FOREWORD

In the inspiring pages of "Portraits of Heroes: 30 Trailblazers in Black History," get ready to discover incredible stories of courage and determination that have shaped our world!

These heroes dared to dream big, fought against unfairness, and made a real difference. They stood tall even when things were tough, showing us all what bravery means.

From Martin Luther King Jr.'s inspiring speeches to Rosa Parks' courageous stand, from Malcolm X's bold ideas to Harriet Tubman's quiet strength, each hero in this book has a special story to tell.

As you read, you'll learn about the struggles they faced and the victories they achieved. You'll see how they each made a mark on history and inspired others to stand up for what's right.

So dive into these stories, and let them inspire you to make a difference too! By learning about Black history, we honor the incredible heroes who came before us and keep their legacy alive.

Martin Luther King Jr.

AMERICAN CHRISTIAN MINISTER & ACTIVIST

Martin Luther King Jr. was a prominent leader in the fight for fairness and equality. He believed that people should be judged by their actions and character, not by the color of their skin. He became famous for his powerful speech called "*I Have a Dream*," where he shared his vision for a world where all people are treated equally.

Dr. King used peaceful methods, such as protests and marches, to stand up against unfair laws and segregation. One of his most famous actions was leading the **Montgomery Bus Boycott**, where people refused to ride buses until the rules were changed to treat everyone fairly.

FUN FACT

- Martin Luther King Jr. loved music and often sang to find strength.
- He skipped two grades in high school and entered college at only 15 years old.

> " Darkness cannot drive out darkness; only light can do that. Hate cannot drive out hate; only love can do that. "

I HAVE A DREAM

MARTIN LUTHER KING JR.

1929
Martin Luther King Jr. was born in Atlanta, Georgia.

1955
Led the **Montgomery Bus Boycott** to fight against racial segregation.

1963
Delivered his famous "**I Have a Dream**" speech during the March on Washington.

1964
Received the **Nobel Peace Prize** for his work in civil rights.

1968
Martin Luther King Jr. was assassinated, but his legacy lives on.

LEGACY

Martin Luther King Jr. dreamed of a world where people of all races live together peacefully. His lasting legacy inspires individuals to fight for justice and to demonstrate love and compassion towards each other.

Rosa Parks

AMERICAN ACTIVIST

Rosa Parks, born on February 4, 1913, was a brave woman who stood up against segregation. She earned the nickname "*Mother of the Civil Rights Movement*" because of her important role in bringing about change.

When she refused to give up her bus seat to a white person, it sparked big changes in the fight against segregation. This small act of defiance became a powerful symbol of resistance.

Rosa Parks' courage inspired many others to stand up for their rights. Her bravery broke down racial barriers and left a lasting impact, encouraging people to speak out against unfairness and fight for equality.

> " The only tired I was, was tired of giving in. "

 **FUN FACT**

- Rosa Parks was a seamstress, and her sewing skills played a role in the Civil Rights Movement.
- She worked with the **NAACP** (National Association for the Advancement of Colored People) to fight for equal rights.

THE COURAGE TO SIT FOR CHANGE

1913
Rosa Parks was born in Tuskegee, Alabama.

1955
Refused to give up her seat on a bus, sparking the *Montgomery Bus Boycott*.

1956
The U.S. Supreme Court decided that it was against the law to separate people on public buses based on their race.

1999
Awarded the *Congressional Gold Medal of Honor*.

2005
Rosa Parks passed away, leaving behind a legacy of courage.

LEGACY

Rosa Parks' bravery inspired others to stand up for their rights. Her actions helped break down racial barriers, and her courage is remembered every time people fight against unfair treatment.

Frederick Douglass

AMERICAN ABOLITIONIST, ORATOR & WRITER

Frederick Douglass, born in 1818, was a symbol of courage and strength in the battle against slavery. He was an abolitionist, which means he fought to end slavery, and he wrote a lot of books and speeches to spread his message of freedom and fairness for everyone.

Douglass used his powerful voice and intelligence to educate people about the terrible realities of slavery and why it was so important for everyone to be free. His hard work and determination reached many people, both in America and beyond, giving hope to those fighting for equality.

 **FUN FACT**

- Frederick Douglass taught himself to read and write, despite the laws against educating enslaved individuals.
- He became one of the most prominent African American leaders of the 19th century and was a key figure in the abolitionist movement.

> " Without a struggle, there can be no progress. "

VOICE FOR FREEDOM

1818
Frederick Douglass was born into slavery in Maryland.

1838
Escaped from slavery and began his journey to freedom in the North.

1845
Published his autobiography, "*Narrative of the Life of Frederick Douglass, an American Slave.*"

1847
Founded "*The North Star*," an abolitionist newspaper that advocated for the end of slavery.

1863
Advised President Abraham Lincoln during the Civil War on matters related to freedom and equality.

1895
Passed away, leaving behind a legacy of activism and inspiration.

LEGACY

Frederick Douglass's teachings about the importance of freedom, equality, and education remain relevant today. His legacy reminds us of the power of perseverance and the importance of standing up for what is right.

Harriet Tubman

AMERICAN ABOLITIONIST & SOCIAL ACTIVIST

Leading the Way to Freedom

Harriet Tubman, born around 1822, was a remarkable woman known as the "***Moses of her people***." She risked her life to help enslaved individuals escape to freedom through the ***Underground Railroad***.

Harriet Tubman's courage and determination saved hundreds of enslaved individuals from bondage. She risked her life time and again to lead others to freedom, never losing faith in her mission.

> I freed a thousand slaves; I could have freed a thousand more if only they knew they were slaves.

 **FUN FACT**

- Harriet Tubman was known by the nickname "***Moses***" because, like the biblical figure, she led her people to freedom.
- She carried a gun during her missions on the Underground Railroad to protect herself and the people she was leading to freedom.

LEADING THE WAY

1822
Harriet Tubman was born into slavery in Maryland.

1849
Escaped from slavery and began her work as a conductor on the *Underground Railroad*.

1850s - 1860s
Led many dangerous missions to guide enslaved people to freedom in the North.

1863
During the Civil War, Harriet Tubman served as a spy and nurse for the Union Army.

1913
Passed away, leaving behind a legacy of bravery and compassion.

LEGACY

Harriet Tubman's fearless leadership and unwavering commitment to justice inspire people to this day. Her legacy serves as a reminder of the power of determination and compassion in the fight for freedom and equality.

Malcolm X

AMERICAN MUSLIM MINISTER & HUMAN RIGHTS ACTIVIST

Malcolm X, born on May 19, 1925, was a passionate advocate for the rights of Black Americans.

His journey from a difficult past to a prominent leadership position showcased the capacity for transformation in everyone, motivating many to fight against racism and inequality.

Fearlessly, he confronted racial discrimination and oppression, calling on society to confront these injustices. He promoted Black pride, self-reliance, and unity in his fight for equality.

 **FUN FACT**

- Malcolm X was an avid reader and self-taught scholar, educating himself while serving time in prison.
- He was a captivating speaker, known for his passionate speeches that inspired many people seeking empowerment.

> " We are nonviolent with people who are nonviolent with us. "

VOICE FOR JUSTICE

1925

Malcolm X was born Malcolm Little in Omaha, Nebraska.

1946

Incarcerated for burglary, Malcolm X begins his transformation through education and self-reflection.

1952

Joins the Nation of Islam and adopts the name *Malcolm X*, signifying his rejection of his "slave name."

1964

Breaks away from the Nation of Islam and embraces orthodox Islam after performing the *Hajj* pilgrimage to Mecca.

1965

Assassinated in New York City, but his legacy lives on as a symbol of resistance and empowerment.

LEGACY

Malcolm X's teachings about self-respect, empowerment, and resistance continue to inspire movements for social justice and equality today. He inspired generations to question authority, seek knowledge, and stand up against injustice.

Maya Angelou

AMERICAN POET & CIVIL RIGHTS ACTIVIST

Maya Angelou, born on April 4, 1928, was a renowned poet, author, and civil rights activist. Her powerful words and unwavering spirit continue to inspire people around the world.

She bravely shared her experiences through her writing, which helped people understand and connect with others' struggles. Her words of wisdom and poetry touched the hearts of many, offering comfort and hope. She also fought for fairness and equality, leaving a lasting impact on the world.

Maya Angelou showed us the power of resilience, compassion, and using our voices for good.

 **FUN FACT**

- Maya Angelou was fluent in several languages, including French, Spanish, and Italian.
- She was a dancer, singer, and actress, appearing in films, television shows, and stage productions.

> " History, despite its wrenching pain, cannot be unlived, but if faced with courage, need not be lived again. "

AND STILL I RISE

1928

Maya Angelou was born **_Marguerite Annie Johnson_** in St. Louis, Missouri.

1940s

Overcame childhood trauma and found comfort in literature and writing.

1969

Published her groundbreaking autobiography, "**_I Know Why the Caged Bird Sings_**."

1993

Became the first African American woman to recite a poem at a presidential inauguration.

2014

Passed away, leaving behind a legacy of resilience and wisdom.

LEGACY

Maya Angelou's legacy as a literary icon and social activist lives on through her timeless words and actions. Her legacy reminds us of the power of storytelling to heal, inspire, and bring people together.

Thurgood Marshall

AMERICAN CIVIL RIGHTS LAWYER

Thurgood Marshall, born on July 2, 1908, was a pioneering attorney and the first African American Supreme Court Justice. His dedication to justice and equality led to significant changes in the American legal system.

He worked tirelessly to ensure that everyone was treated fairly under the law, and his legal victories played a crucial role in ending segregation and promoting fairness in America.

Marshall's unwavering commitment to promoting justice served as an inspiration for many, especially lawyers and activists dedicated to advocating for fairness and equality.

FUN FACT

- Thurgood Marshall was an exceptional student who graduated at the top of his class from Howard University School of Law.
- He had a sharp wit and was known for his clever courtroom arguments and quick comebacks.

> " In recognizing the humanity of our fellow beings, we pay ourselves the highest tribute. "

JUSTICE FOR ALL

1908
Thurgood Marshall was born in Baltimore, Maryland.

1930s - 1940s
Championed civil rights as a lawyer for the **NAACP** (National Association for the Advancement of Colored People).

1954
Successfully argued the landmark case **Brown v. Board of Education**, leading to the desegregation of public schools.

1967
Became the first African American Supreme Court Justice, serving with distinction until 1991.

1993
Passed away, leaving behind a legacy of legal brilliance and advocacy.

LEGACY

Thurgood Marshall's legacy lives on in the ongoing struggle for equality and justice. His courage, intellect, and unwavering commitment to fairness continue to inspire people around the world.

Nelson Mandela

SOUTH AFRICAN ANTI-APARTHEID ACTIVIST & POLITICIAN

A Champion of Freedom.

Nelson Mandela, born on July 18, 1918, was a courageous leader who dedicated his life to fighting against *apartheid* in South Africa. His resilience, forgiveness, and commitment to justice made him a global symbol of peace and reconciliation.

Nelson Mandela's unwavering commitment to justice and equality helped end apartheid and usher in a new era of democracy in South Africa. He believed in the power of forgiveness and reconciliation to heal the wounds of the past.

 **FUN FACT**

- Nelson Mandela was an avid boxer in his youth and embraced physical fitness throughout his life.
- He was awarded the *Nobel Peace Prize* in 1993 for his efforts to dismantle apartheid and promote peace.

> " It always seems impossible until it's done. "

CHAMPION OF FREEDOM

1918
Nelson Mandela was born in the village of Mvezo, South Africa.

1944
Joined the African National Congress (**ANC**) to fight against racial segregation.

1962
Arrested and sentenced to life in prison for his anti-apartheid activism.

1990
Released from prison after 27 years, sparking hope for a new era of democracy in South Africa.

1994
Elected as South Africa's first black president in the country's first democratic elections.

2013
Passed away, leaving behind a legacy of forgiveness and unity.

LEGACY

Nelson Mandela's teachings about reconciliation, forgiveness, and the importance of human rights remain relevant today. His legacy inspires people to strive for a fair and equal society.

W.E.B. Du Bois

AMERICAN SCHOLAR & CIVIL RIGHTS ACTIVIST

A Champion of Equality.

W.E.B. Du Bois, born on February 23, 1868, was a pioneering sociologist, historian, and civil rights advocate. His brilliance, activism, and dedication to racial equality paved the way for the civil rights movement in the United States.

Through his scholarly work and activism, Du Bois confronted racism and injustice with determination. He tirelessly used his influence to advocate for civil rights, promote education, and push for social equality for African Americans.

 **FUN FACT**

- W.E.B. Du Bois was a prolific writer and editor, contributing to numerous publications and scholarly journals.
- He passionately advocated for ***Pan-Africanism***, firmly believing in the unity and solidarity of people of African descent across the globe.

> " The worker must work for the glory of his handiwork, not simply for pay; the thinker must think for truth, not for fame. "

PIONEER OF EQUALITY

1868

W.E.B. Du Bois was born in Great Barrington, Massachusetts.

1895

Became the first African American to earn a Ph.D. from Harvard University.

1909

Co-founded the National Association for the Advancement of Colored People to fight against racial discrimination.

1903

Published "*The Souls of Black Folk*," an influential book on African American identity and the struggle for equality.

1963

Joined the March on Washington and met with Martin Luther King Jr.

1963

Passed away, leaving behind a legacy of scholarship and activism.

LEGACY

W.E.B. Du Bois's ideas about racial equality, education, and social justice still matter today. His groundbreaking research and civil rights advocacy remind us of the importance of fairness and ensuring equal access to education for everyone.

Elizabeth Freeman

A BRAVE WOMAN

A Trailblazer for Freedom.

Elizabeth Freeman, also known as **Mum Bett**, was a courageous woman who played a significant role in the fight against slavery in the United States. Her bravery and determination made her a symbol of freedom and justice.

Her successful lawsuit for her freedom questioned the legality of slavery in Massachusetts and contributed to the eventual abolition of slavery in the state. Her actions helped pave the way for freedom and equality for countless others.

 **FUN FACT**

- Elizabeth Freeman learned to read and write, despite laws prohibiting the education of enslaved individuals.
- After gaining her freedom, she worked as a paid servant and became a beloved member of the Sedgwick family, where she lived until her passing.

> " I heard that paper read yesterday, that says all men are created equal, and that every man has a right to freedom. I'm not a dumb critter; won't the law give me my freedom? "

TRAILBLAZER FOR FREEDOM

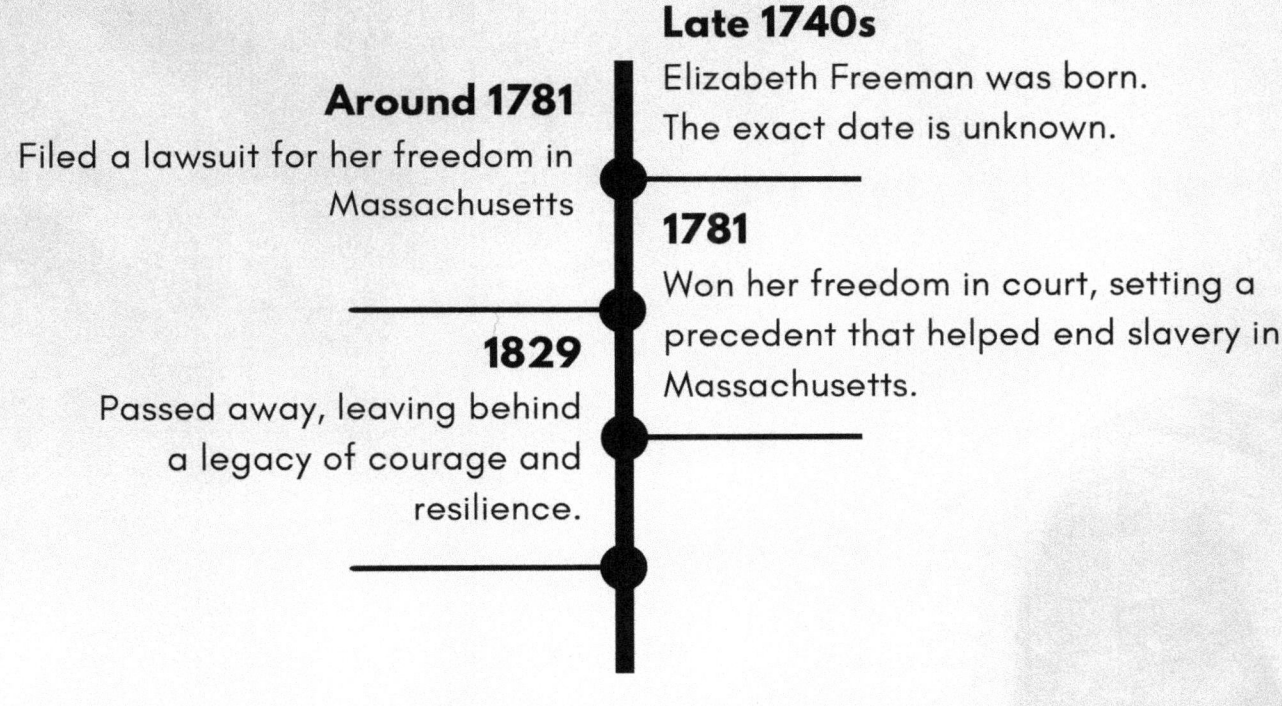

Late 1740s
Elizabeth Freeman was born. The exact date is unknown.

Around 1781
Filed a lawsuit for her freedom in Massachusetts

1781
Won her freedom in court, setting a precedent that helped end slavery in Massachusetts.

1829
Passed away, leaving behind a legacy of courage and resilience.

LEGACY

Elizabeth Freeman's courageous fight for freedom is a reminder of the resilience and strength of enslaved individuals who dared to challenge the institution of slavery. Her legacy continues to inspire those fighting for justice and equality today.

Shirley Chisolm

AMERICAN EDUCATOR & POLITICIAN

Shirley Chisholm, born on November 30, 1924, was a trailblazing politician and educator. She made history as the first African American woman elected to the United States Congress and later became the first African American to run for a major party's nomination for President of the United States.

Shirley Chisholm's groundbreaking political career paved the way for future generations of women and people of color to pursue leadership roles in government. She fearlessly advocated for the rights of marginalized communities and fought for fairer policies that would benefit everyone.

 **FUN FACT**

- Shirley Chisholm was a founding member of both the Congressional Black Caucus and the National Women's Political Caucus.
- She authored two books: **"Unbought and Unbossed"** and **"The Good Fight."**

> " If they don't give you a seat at the table, bring a folding chair. "

UNBOUGHT & UNBOSSED

1924

Shirley Chisholm was born in Brooklyn, New York.

1968

Elected to the U.S. House of Representatives, representing New York's 12th congressional district.

1972

Announced her historic campaign for the Democratic nomination for President of the United States.

1983

Retired from Congress after serving seven terms, leaving behind a legacy of courage and advocacy.

2005

Passed away, but her legacy as a champion for equality and social justice lives on.

LEGACY

Shirley Chisolm's legacy reminds us of the importance of representation, diversity, and inclusion in leadership positions. Her boldness, integrity, and commitment to justice serve as a beacon of hope for those fighting for equality and representation.

Barack Obama

AMERICAN POLITICIAN

Barack Obama, born on August 4, 1961, made history as the first African American President of the United States. His leadership, charisma, and message of hope inspired millions around the world.

Barack Obama's presidency marked a historic moment in American history. He successfully steered the country through economic crisis, expanded healthcare access with the **Affordable Care Act**, and championed progressive policies on climate change, LGBTQ+ rights, and immigration reform.

 **FUN FACT**

- Barack Obama is an avid basketball player and a big fan of the sport.
- He is also an accomplished author, with bestselling memoirs like "***Dreams from My Father***" and "***The Audacity of Hope***."

> Change will not come if we wait for some other person or some other time. We are the ones we've been waiting for. We are the change that we seek.

HOPE & CHANGE

1961
Barack Obama was born in Honolulu, Hawaii.

1988
Graduated from Harvard Law School and became the first African American president of the Harvard Law Review.

1996
Elected to the Illinois State Senate, he served for eight years, championing social justice & healthcare reforms.

2008
Elected as the 44th President of the United States, promising hope and change.

2012
Reelected for a second term, continuing his efforts to improve healthcare, address climate change, and promote equality.

LEGACY

Barack Obama's legacy as a transformative leader and symbol of progress and unity continues to inspire people around the world. His presidency shattered racial barriers and renewed faith in the American dream.

Booker T. Washington

AMERICAN EDUCATOR, AUTHOR & ORATOR

Booker T. Washington, born on April 5, 1856, was a well-known educator, writer, and civil rights advocate. He spent his life working to better the lives of African Americans through education and vocational training.

Washington's leadership and ideas changed how African American education was viewed in the United States. He thought that economic independence and being able to rely on oneself were key parts of making progress for Black people.

FUN FACT

- Booker T. Washington was a skilled orator and advisor to several U.S. presidents, including Theodore Roosevelt and William Howard Taft.
- He was a proponent of the "***Atlanta Compromise***," advocating for African American economic advancement through vocational education & entrepreneurship.

> Success is to be measured not so much by the position that one has reached in life as by the obstacles which he has overcome.

SELF RELIANCE

1856

Booker T. Washington was born into slavery on a plantation in Virginia.

1865

Enslaved during his early childhood, Booker and his family were emancipated after the Civil War.

1872

Enrolled at what is known now as Hampton University, where he worked and studied to support his education.

1881

Founded what is known now as Tuskegee University, emphasizing practical skills and vocational training for African Americans.

1901

Published his autobiography, "***Up from Slavery***," detailing his journey from enslavement to educational leadership.

1915

Passed away, leaving behind a legacy of educational empowerment and advocacy.

LEGACY

Booker T. Washington's emphasis on education, self-reliance, and economic empowerment remains relevant today. His teachings continue to inspire discussions on racial equality and the importance of access to quality education.

Sojourner Truth

AMERICAN ABOLITIONIST

Sojourner Truth, born into slavery around 1797 as Isabella Baumfree, was a remarkable abolitionist, women's rights activist, and preacher. Her powerful speeches and unwavering commitment to equality made her an influential figure in the fight against slavery and discrimination.

Truth's bravery and powerful words motivated many to stand up against slavery and injustice. She fearlessly confronted those in power and devoted her life to advocating for fairness and equality for everyone.

> If the first woman God ever made was strong enough to turn the world upside down all alone, these women together ought to be able to turn it back, and get it right side up again!

 **FUN FACT**

- Sojourner Truth was over six feet tall, and her commanding presence added to the impact of her speeches.
- She taught herself to read and write and became known for her powerful storytelling abilities.

VOICE FOR FREEDOM

Around 1797

Sojourner Truth is born into slavery in New York, as *Isabella Baumfree*.

1826

Escapes slavery with her infant daughter, finding refuge with a Quaker family.

1843

Takes the name *Sojourner Truth* and begins her work as a preacher, advocating for abolition and women's rights.

1851

Delivers her famous speech, "*Ain't I a Woman?*" at the Women's Rights Convention in Akron, Ohio

1863

Meets President Abraham Lincoln and advocates for African American soldiers and the abolition of slavery.

1883

Publishes her autobiography, "*The Narrative of Sojourner Truth*," recounting her life and experiences.

LEGACY

Sojourner Truth's legacy as a champion of human rights and dignity continues to inspire people around the world. Her courageous advocacy laid the groundwork for future generations of activists fighting for justice and equality.

Langston Hughes

AMERICAN POET & SOCIAL ACTIVIST

Langston Hughes, born on February 1, 1902, was a celebrated poet, playwright, and activist. His powerful writings captured the spirit of the **Harlem Renaissance** and continue to inspire readers around the world.

Langston Hughes's poetry explored themes of identity, equality, and what it means to be African American. His poems are loved by people from all walks of life and are still appreciated today for their beauty and importance.

 **FUN FACT**

- Langston Hughes was a prolific writer who published poetry, novels, essays, plays, and children's books.
- He traveled extensively, lecturing and performing his poetry around the world.

> " Let America be America again. Let it be the dream it used to be. "

HARLEM RENAISSANCE

1902

Langston Hughes was born in Joplin, Missouri.

1921

Enrolled at Columbia University but left after one year to pursue his writing career in Harlem, New York.

1926

Published his first collection of poetry, "*The Weary Blues*," which garnered critical acclaim.

1930s - 1940s

Became a leading figure of the *Harlem Renaissance*, a movement that celebrated African American art, literature, & music.

1967

Passed away, leaving behind a legacy of literary excellence and social activism.

LEGACY

Langston Hughes's impact on African American literature and culture is unmatched. His contributions helped bring the voices of Black writers and artists to the forefront, inspiring countless individuals to follow their creative dreams.

Carter G. Woodson

AMERICAN HISTORIAN & AUTHOR

Carter G. Woodson, born on December 19, 1875, was a groundbreaking historian, teacher, and writer. He dedicated his life to promoting the study and celebration of African American history and culture.

Woodson's work was instrumental in enlightening people about the genuine achievements and stories of African Americans, which had often been overlooked. He helped start the academic study of African American history and culture, laying the groundwork for future generations to learn and celebrate their heritage.

 **FUN FACT**

- Carter G. Woodson worked as a coal miner to support his education and later became a distinguished educator and scholar.
- He authored numerous books, including **"*The Mis-Education of the Negro*"** and **"*The Negro in Our History*,"** which are still widely read today.

> " Those who have no record of what their forebears have accomplished lose the inspiration which comes from the teaching of biography and history. "

FATHER OF BLACK HISTORY

1875

Carter G. Woodson was born to formerly enslaved parents in Virginia.

1907

Earned his bachelor's degree from Berea College in Kentucky.

1912

Completed his PhD in history from Harvard University, the second African American to earn a doctorate from Harvard.

1915

Founded what is known now as the Association for the Study of African American Life and History.

1926

Established *Negro History Week*, which later evolved into *Black History Month*.

1950

Passed away, but his legacy as a pioneer of African American history education lives on.

LEGACY

Carter G. Woodson's vision for fair and inclusive history education reminds us that everyone's story matters. He thought it was essential to teach African American history in schools, and because of his determination, it's now a crucial part of American history lessons.

Muhammad Ali

AMERICAN BOXER & ACTIVIST

Muhammad Ali, born **Cassius Marcellus Clay Jr.** on January 17, 1942, was one of the most iconic and influential athletes of the 20th century. Beyond his legendary boxing career, he was known for his activism, charisma, and unwavering commitment to his beliefs.

Mohammad Ali's influence went far beyond just sports. He used his fame to speak out against racism, injustice, and war, inspiring millions around the world to stand up for their beliefs and fight for change.

 **FUN FACT**

- Muhammad Ali was famous for being really clever and funny. He had a quick wit and a charming personality, and he was known for saying catchy rhymes and memorable one-liners.
- He was also a dedicated humanitarian, traveling the world to promote peace, humanitarian causes, and diplomacy.

> " Float like a butterfly, sting like a bee. The hands can't hit what the eyes can't see. "

GREATEST OF ALL TIME

1942
Muhammad Ali was born
in Louisville, Kentucky.

1960
Won a gold medal in boxing
at the Summer Olympics in
Rome, Italy.

1964
Defeated Sonny Liston to become the
heavyweight champion of the world
and announced his conversion to Islam

1967
Refused to be drafted into the Vietnam War,
citing religious and moral objections, and as a
result, he was stripped of his boxing titles.

1971
Regained his heavyweight title
by defeating Joe Frazier in the
"*Fight of the Century*."

1981
Retired from professional
boxing with a record of 56
wins and 5 losses.

2016
Passed away, leaving behind a legacy
of courage, resilience, and activism.

LEGACY

Muhammad Ali's impact goes way beyond just boxing. His example of using fame and
influence for social change continues to inspire athletes, activists, and ordinary people to
fight for justice and equality.

Madam C. J. Walker

AMERICAN ENTREPRENEUR, PHILANTHROPIST & ACTIVIST

Madam C.J. Walker, born *Sarah Breedlove* on December 23, 1867, was an amazing entrepreneur, philanthropist, and advocate for empowering African Americans. She created innovative hair care products and was incredibly talented in running her business, which made her one of the richest self-made women in America.

Her achievements as a businesswoman and her generosity broke down barriers based on race and gender. She used her wealth and influence to uplift her community and advocate for change, paving the way for future generations of African American entrepreneurs.

 **FUN FACT**

- She is recorded as the first female self-made millionaire in America in the *Guinness Book of World Records*.
- She was a trailblazer in the use of marketing and branding techniques, sending salespeople directly to people's doors and creating clever ads that got attention.

> " I got my start by giving myself a start "

PIONEER OF ENTREPRENEURSHIP

1867
Madam C.J. Walker was born to formerly enslaved parents in Delta, Louisiana.

Late 1880s
Faced with hair loss, she experimented with homemade remedies, eventually creating her own "Walker System" formula.

1905
Founded the Madam C.J. Walker Manufacturing Company, specializing in hair care products for African American women.

1910
Established the Madam C.J. Walker Beauty Culture School in Pittsburgh, training sales agents and hair stylists.

1913
Built *Villa Lewaro*, a luxurious estate in New York, becoming one of the first African American women to own such a property.

1919
Passed away, but her legacy as a trailblazing entrepreneur and philanthropist lives on.

LEGACY

Madam C.J. Walker's impact on business, beauty, and social activism is felt to this day. Her journey from poverty to prosperity demonstrates how determination, resilience, and believing in yourself can lead to great achievements.

Jackie Robinson

AMERICAN BASEBALL PLAYER

Jackie Robinson, born on January 31, 1919, was a groundbreaking athlete and civil rights activist who changed the game of baseball forever. By breaking the color barrier in *Major League Baseball*, his bravery and talent opened doors for racial equality in professional sports and beyond, leaving a lasting impact on future generations.

Jackie's courage and skill were not limited to the baseball field. He also used his fame to speak out for civil rights and fairness, standing up against segregation and showing incredible composure in the face of challenges. His actions inspired millions of people and continue to be remembered as symbols of strength and resilience.

 **FUN FACT**

- Jackie Robinson was a talented athlete in multiple sports, excelling in baseball, football, basketball, and track and field.
- After retiring from baseball, he continued his activism, working to promote equality and justice in various ways.

> " A life is not important except in the impact it has on other lives. "

BREAKING BARRIERS

1919

Jackie Robinson was born in Cairo, Georgia.

1947

Signed by the **Brooklyn Dodgers**, becoming the first African American to play in Major League Baseball in the modern era.

1947

Despite facing racism and discrimination, Robinson excelled on the field, winning the inaugural **Rookie of the Year** Award.

1949

Became the first African American to win the National League Most Valuable Player (**MVP**) Award

1955

Helped lead the Dodgers to victory in the World Series, earning his only championship title.

1962

Inducted into the **Baseball Hall of Fame**, forever cementing his legacy as one of the greatest players in baseball history.

1972

Passed away, but his impact on sports and society continues to be felt to this day.

LEGACY

Jackie Robinson's legacy as a trailblazer and cultural icon is very significant in American history. His influence on sports and society reaches far beyond his lifetime, serving as a reminder of the importance of perseverance, integrity, and courage.

Oprah Winfrey

AMERICAN HOST & TELEVISION PRODUCER

Oprah Winfrey, born on January 29, 1954, is widely recognized as a groundbreaking media figure, philanthropist, and advocate for social change. Her influential talk show, business ventures, and charitable work have earned her a place among the most respected and admired women worldwide.

Her impact on media and culture is immense. Through her talk show, books, movies, and charitable activities, she has touched the lives of millions, inspiring them to live their best lives and make a positive difference in the world.

 **FUN FACT**

- Oprah Winfrey is an accomplished actress, producer, and author, having appeared in several films and television shows and written multiple best-selling books.
- She is also a passionate advocate for causes such as education, healthcare, and human rights, using her fame to create positive change.

> " Turn your wounds into wisdom. "

MEDIA MOGUL

1954

Oprah Winfrey is born into poverty in rural Mississippi.

1986

Launches "*The Oprah Winfrey Show*," which becomes the highest-rated talk show in television history, running for 25 seasons.

1986

Becomes the first African American woman to own her own television studio, *Harpo Studios*, in Chicago.

1998

Establishes the *Oprah Winfrey Foundation* to support education, empowerment, and advocacy for women and children.

2011

Launches the Oprah Winfrey Network (*OWN*), a multimedia platform dedicated to uplifting and inspiring programming.

Continues to use her platform to promote social justice, wellness, and personal growth through various initiatives.

LEGACY

Oprah Winfrey's journey from poverty to success is a story of hope, proving that anything is possible with hard work, determination, and compassion. Her commitment to empowering others and promoting positive change inspires people worldwide to pursue their dreams and make a difference in their communities.

Arthur Ashe

AMERICAN TENNIS PLAYER

Arthur Ashe, born on July 10, 1943, was a trailblazing tennis player, activist, and humanitarian. He broke barriers as the first African American to win major tennis championships and used his platform to advocate for social justice and equality.

His impact on tennis and society went beyond sports. He used his platform to challenge racial barriers, advocate for equality, and promote education and healthcare initiatives.

 **FUN FACT**

- Arthur Ashe was not only a talented athlete but also an accomplished scholar, graduating from the University of California, Los Angeles (UCLA), with a degree in business administration.
- He was a committed advocate for civil rights and participated in protests against apartheid in South Africa.

> " Start where you are. Use what you have. Do what you can. "

TENNIS CHAMPION & ACTIVIST

1943

Arthur Ashe was born in Richmond, Virginia.

1968

Becomes the first African American to win the *U.S. Open* singles title, a historic achievement that solidified his place in tennis history.

1975

Wins the *Wimbledon* men's singles championship, further cementing his status as one of the greatest tennis players of all time.

1988

Announces his HIV diagnosis, becoming an advocate for AIDS awareness and research.

1992

Establishes the Arthur Ashe Foundation for the Defeat of AIDS to support AIDS education and research initiatives.

1993

Passed away from AIDS-related complications, but his legacy as a champion of tennis and social justice lives on.

LEGACY

Arthur Ashe's dedication to social justice, education, and healthcare is an inspiration for people to drive change in their communities. His focus on excellence, integrity, and service highlights how sports can influence positive changes.

Fannie Lou Hamer

AMERICAN ACTIVIST

Fannie Lou Hamer, born on October 6, 1917, was a courageous civil rights leader and advocate for voting rights. Despite enduring oppression and violence, she remained committed to her fight for equality and empowering African Americans to participate in the democratic process through voting.

Her courage and determination helped push the civil rights movement forward and made sure African Americans could vote without facing discrimination. Her efforts led to the passing of the **Voting Rights Act** of 1965, which made it against the law to treat people unfairly because of their race when voting.

 **FUN FACT**

- Fannie Lou Hamer was known for her powerful singing voice and often used music as a tool for activism and empowerment.
- She co-founded the **Freedom Farm Cooperative**, which provided housing and economic opportunities for African American farmers in Mississippi.

> "Sometimes it seem like to tell the truth today is to run the risk of being killed. But if I fall, I'll fall five feet four inches forward in the fight for freedom. I'm not backing off."

RIGHT TO VOTE FOR ALL

1917
Fannie Lou Hamer is born in Montgomery County, Mississippi.

1962
Attends a voter registration workshop and becomes active in the civil rights movement

1964
Co-founds the Mississippi Freedom Democratic Party (**MFDP**) to fight for African American representation.

1964
Testifies at the Democratic National Convention about her experiences facing voter suppression and violence.

1968
Runs for Congress, paving the way for future generations of African American politicians.

1977
Passed away, but her legacy as a tireless advocate for civil rights and voting rights lives on.

LEGACY

Fannie Lou Hamer's legacy inspires people to keep working towards a fairer and more equal society for everyone. Her bravery when faced with challenges reminds us of how powerful it is when people come together and take action to make a difference.

Medgar Evers

AMERICAN CIVIL RIGHTS ACTIVIST

Medgar Evers, born on July 2, 1925, was a courageous civil rights activist who dedicated his life to fighting racial segregation and injustice. His work to enhance civil and voting rights in Mississippi made him a target of violence by white supremacists, ultimately leading to his tragic death.

Evers played a crucial role in the civil rights movement, advocating for desegregation, voting rights, and equal opportunities in education and employment. His courage and sacrifice continue to inspire activists striving for fairness and equality today.

 **FUN FACT**

- Medgar Evers was a talented athlete and won a scholarship to attend Alcorn State University, where he earned a degree in business administration.
- He worked tirelessly to investigate and document incidents of racial violence and discrimination in Mississippi, often at great personal risk.

> " You can kill a man, but you can't kill an idea. "

CIVIL RIGHTS & MARTYRDOM

1925

Medgar Evers is born in Decatur, Mississippi.

1943

Enlists in the United States Army and serves in World War II, experiencing racial discrimination and segregation in the military.

1954

Becomes NAACP's first field secretary in Mississippi, organizing voter drives and leading boycotts against segregation.

1963

Helps James Meredith integrate the University of Mississippi, facing violent resistance from segregationists.

1963

Assassinated in front of his home in Jackson, Mississippi, by a white supremacist.

1964

Byron De La Beckwith, Evers' assassin, is arrested and charged with murder, but two all-white juries deadlock, resulting in mistrials.

1994

Beckwith is finally convicted of Evers' murder, more than 30 years after the crime.

LEGACY

Medgar Evers' assassination shocked the nation and brought renewed support for the civil rights movement. His sacrifice helped bring national attention to the struggle for racial equality and inspired a new generation of activists to continue the fight.

Ruby Bridges

AMERICAN CIVIL RIGHTS ACTIVIST

Ruby Bridges, born on September 8, 1954, is a symbol of courage and resilience in the fight against racial segregation. At just six years old, she became the first African American student to integrate an all-white elementary school in the South, paving the way for future generations of students.

Her bravery and determination helped advance the cause of civil rights and brought national attention to the struggle against segregation in schools. Her courage in the face of adversity continues to inspire generations.

 **FUN FACT**

- Ruby Bridges' integration of **William Frantz Elementary School** was depicted in the famous painting "*The Problem We All Live With*" by Norman Rockwell.
- She later became an activist and advocate for education, working to promote racial equality and diversity in schools.

> " Each and every one of us is born with a clean heart. Our babies know nothing about hate or racism. But soon they begin to learn - and only from us. We keep racism alive. We pass it on to our children. "

PIONEER OF INTEGRATION

1954

Ruby Bridges is born in Tylertown, Mississippi.

1960

Enrolls at William Frantz Elementary School in New Orleans, Louisiana, as part of the court-ordered integration of public schools.

1960

Faces hostility and threats from white protesters as she walks to school each day, escorted by federal marshals.

1960

Attends school alone for the entire year, as white parents refuse to allow their children to attend school with her.

1999

Receives the Presidential Citizens Medal from President Bill Clinton for her role in advancing civil rights.

2011

The children's book "***Ruby Bridges Goes to School: My True Story***" is published, sharing her experience with young readers.

Continues to advocate for equality and education, sharing her story to inspire others to stand up against injustice.

LEGACY

Ruby Bridges' impact on the fight for racial equality and social justice demonstrates the incredible influence one individual can have. Her journey as a young pioneer of integration serves as a powerful reminder of the importance of standing up against injustice and fighting for equality.

Marcus Garvey

JAMAICAN ACTIVIST

Marcus Garvey, born on August 17, 1887, was a leader with bold visions who advocated for the rights of people of African descent across the globe. His belief in unity among Africans and the importance of being economically independent inspired millions and helped start the civil rights movement.

Garvey's ideas about Africans coming together and being in control of their destinies meant a lot to many people. He also believed in being proud of being black, working hard to be financially independent, and relying on oneself. These ideas provided the foundation for the civil rights and black power movements of the 20th century.

 **FUN FACT**

- Marcus Garvey was a prolific writer and orator, publishing newspapers and pamphlets advocating for black empowerment and liberation.
- He envisioned a "***Back to Africa***" movement, urging people of African descent to return to their ancestral homeland and build a new society free from colonialism and oppression.

> " Up, you mighty race, accomplish what you will. "

BLACK EMPOWERMENT

1887

Marcus Garvey is born in St. Ann's Bay, Jamaica.

1914

Founds *UNIA* in Jamaica, with the goal of uniting people of African descent and promoting racial pride and self-reliance.

1916

Moves to the United States and establishes branches of the UNIA in Harlem, New York, and other cities, attracting thousands of followers.

1920

Holds the first International Convention of the Negro Peoples of the World in New York City.

1920

Launches the Black Star Line, a shipping company aimed at facilitating trade and transportation among people of African descent.

1927

Is convicted of mail fraud and sentenced to prison, but later deported to Jamaica.

1940

Passes away in London, England, but his legacy as a champion of black liberation lives on.

LEGACY

Marcus Garvey's ideas and philosophy still impact racial justice and empowerment movements today. His legacy reminds us how crucial it is for individuals to determine their futures and also work together for equality.

Ida B. Wells

AMERICAN JOURNALIST & EDUCATOR

Ida B. Wells, born on July 16, 1862, was a brave journalist, civil rights activist, and outspoken fighter against racial injustice. Her eye-opening investigative reports on lynching in America revealed the harsh realities of racism and inspired a call for change.

Her courageous journalism and activism shed light on the widespread problem of lynching in America and sparked movements to end racial violence and discrimination. Her work set the stage for the civil rights movement and continues to motivate activists working for justice today.

 **FUN FACT**

- Ida B. Wells was also a co-founder of the National Association for the Advancement of Colored People (NAACP) and a leader in the suffragette movement, advocating for women's right to vote.
- She traveled extensively throughout the United States and abroad, speaking out against lynching and racial injustice.

> " The way to right wrongs is to turn the light of truth upon them. "

FEARLESS CRUSADER

1862

Ida B. Wells is born into slavery in Holly Springs, Mississippi.

1884

Refuses to give up her seat on a train and is forcibly removed, sparking her activism against racial discrimination.

1889

Co-owns and becomes editor of the Memphis Free Speech and Headlight newspaper, using her platform to expose the horrors of lynching

1892

Investigates and publishes her findings on the lynching of three African American men in Memphis, leading to threats against her life and the destruction of her newspaper's office.

1898

Publishes "*Southern Horrors: Lynch Law in All Its Phases*," a pamphlet exposing the true motives behind lynching and calling for an end to the practice..

1931

Passes away, but her legacy as a trailblazing journalist and civil rights leader lives on.

LEGACY

Ida B. Wells' legacy as a trailblazing journalist and civil rights advocate remains a source of inspiration for generations. Her bold endeavors to expose and confront racial violence serve as a reminder of the power of journalism and activism in the fight for equality and justice.

George Washington Carver

AMERICAN SCIENTIST & INVENTOR

George Washington Carver, born in 1864, was an extraordinary scientist and educator who overcame adversity to become one of the most influential figures in agricultural history.

His groundbreaking research into crop rotation and other agricultural innovations changed farming practices and improved the lives of farmers across the United States.

 **FUN FACT**

- Despite facing discrimination and limited access to education, Carver went on to earn multiple degrees in agriculture and science.
- He was a deeply spiritual man and often credited his success to his faith in God and his belief in the power of nature.

> " Education is the key to unlock the golden door of freedom. "

EDUCATION & INNOVATION

1864

George Washington Carver is born into slavery in Diamond, Missouri.

1871

Freed from slavery following the end of the Civil War, Carver pursues an education against all odds.

1896

Becomes the head of the Agriculture Department at the Tuskegee Institute, where he develops innovative farming techniques.

1916

Testifies before Congress on the importance of agriculture and soil conservation, advocating for policies to support small farmers.

1920s - 1930s

Conducts research into the peanut and sweet potato, developing hundreds of uses for these crops, including peanut butter, cosmetics, and dyes.

1943

Passes away, leaving behind a legacy of innovation and service to agriculture and education.

LEGACY

George Washington Carver's commitment to making life better for others still influences how we farm today and encourages scientific research as a tool for change. His focus on sustainability, new ideas, and helping communities serves as a model for addressing modern issues in farming and education.

Zora Neale Hurston

AMERICAN AUTHOR

Zora Neale Hurston, born on January 7, 1891, was a remarkable writer, anthropologist, and key figure of the Harlem Renaissance. Her groundbreaking works celebrated the richness of African American culture and folklore, leaving a lasting impact on American literature and cultural studies.

Zora Neale Hurston's literary works and research played a crucial role in preserving and celebrating African American culture and folklore. Her vivid storytelling and deep understanding of people continue to captivate readers and scholars alike.

 **FUN FACT**

- Zora Neale Hurston was famous for her lively personality and exceptional storytelling abilities, frequently captivating friends and colleagues with anecdotes from her childhood in Eatonville.
- She was a contemporary of writers like Langston Hughes and Alice Walker and regarded them as her friends and collaborators.

> Sometimes, I feel discriminated against, but it does not make me angry. It merely astonishes me. How can any deny themselves the pleasure of my company? It's beyond me.

HARLEM RENAISSANCE ICON

1891

Born in Notasulga, Alabama, and raised in Eatonville, Florida, one of the first all-black towns in the United States.

1925

Publishes her first short story in "*Opportunity*" magazine, launching her literary career

1927

Earns a scholarship to Barnard College, where she studies anthropology under Franz Boas, one of the leading anthropologists of the time.

1937

Publishes her seminal work, "*Their Eyes Were Watching God*," a groundbreaking novel that explores themes of race, gender, and identity in the American South.

1940s - 1950s

Conducts research in the Caribbean and the American South, collecting folklore and documenting African American culture.

1960

Passes away, but her works gained renewed popularity during the Civil Rights Movement.

LEGACY

Zora Neale Hurston's legacy as a celebrated author and cultural historian still shines brightly today. Her stories and research are loved by many readers and studied by scholars, shedding light on the diverse experiences of African American life in the early 20th century.

Ella Fitzgerald

AMERICAN JAZZ SINGER

Ella Fitzgerald, born on April 25, 1917, was a jazz singer who left an unforgettable mark on 20th-century music. She earned the title "*First Lady of Song*" for her mesmerizing voice and unique singing style that wowed audiences worldwide.

Fitzgerald soared to stardom as one of the most iconic singers of her time. Her live performances were described as magical, as she effortlessly improvised and crafted songs on the spot, leaving audiences in awe. Even today, her influence resonates across the music industry, inspiring countless singers who aspire to follow in her footsteps.

 **FUN FACT**

- Ella Fitzgerald had an amazing voice that could sing in a wide range, going from deep and smooth to high and powerful with ease.
- She recorded over 200 albums and won a total of 14 Grammy Awards throughout her career.

> Just don't give up trying to do what you really want to do. Where there is love and inspiration, I don't think you can go wrong.

FIRST LADY OF SONG

1917

Ella Fitzgerald is born in Newport News, Virginia.

1934

Wins a talent contest at the Apollo Theater in Harlem, launching her career in show business

1938

Records her first hit single, "*A-Tisket, A-Tasket*," with the Chick Webb Orchestra, marking the beginning of her solo career.

1956

Becomes the first African American woman to win a Grammy Award for her album "*Ella Fitzgerald Sings the Cole Porter Song Book*."

1958

Releases "*Ella Fitzgerald Sings the Duke Ellington Song Book*," solidifying her reputation as one of the greatest interpreters of jazz standards.

1996

Passes away, leaving behind a legacy of timeless music and artistry.

LEGACY

Ella Fitzgerald's impact can be heard in the music of many artists across different styles of music. Her creative way of singing jazz and her ability to connect with listeners on a deep emotional level still inspire singers and musicians today.

John Lewis

AMERICAN POLITICIAN & CIVIL RIGHTS ACTIVIST

John Lewis, born on February 21, 1940, was a brave civil rights activist and politician who spent his life fighting for equality and justice through peaceful protest. His unwavering dedication to fairness and his fearless support for civil rights still motivate people everywhere.

His bold leadership and belief in peaceful protest were crucial in moving civil rights forward in America. His efforts led to important changes such as securing voting rights for African Americans and inspired many others to keep working for justice.

 **FUN FACT**

- John Lewis was the youngest speaker at the ***March on Washington*** in 1963, where he delivered his iconic speech calling for racial equality and justice.
- He was awarded the ***Presidential Medal of Freedom***, the nation's highest civilian honor, in 2011 by President Barack Obama.

> " When you see something that is not right, not fair, not just, you have to speak up. You have to say something; you have to do something. "

CHAMPION OF JUSTICE

1940

John Lewis is born in Troy, Alabama.

1961

Joins the **Freedom Rides**, challenging segregation on interstate buses and enduring violence and arrests in the fight for civil rights.

1963

Becomes one of the "**Big Six**" leaders of the civil rights movement and helps organize the historic March on Washington, where he delivers a powerful speech calling for racial justice.

1965

Leads the march for voting rights, known as "**Bloody Sunday**," where he is brutally beaten by state troopers.

1987

Elected to the **United States House of Representatives**, a position he holds until his passing.

2020

Passes away on July 17, leaving behind a legacy of courage, integrity, and service to humanity.

LEGACY

John Lewis is remembered as a hero for justice and equality in American history. His lifelong commitment to peaceful protest and his tireless fight for civil rights still inspire people worldwide to stand up against unfairness and work for a better future.

APPENDIX

NAACP	National Association for the Advancement of Colored People/ An organization advocating for civil rights and equality for Black people.
Montgomery Bus Boycott	This was a protest against segregated seating on buses in Montgomery, Alabama. Led by Rosa Parks and Martin Luther King Jr., it marked a significant moment in the civil rights movement.
Civil Rights Movement	A social movement in the United States aimed at ending racial segregation and discrimination against Black Americans.
Abolitionist Movement	A movement to end slavery in the United States. Abolitionists worked to outlaw slavery and grant freedom to enslaved individuals.
Suffrage Movement	A movement advocating for the right to vote, particularly for women.
Underground Railroad	A network of secret routes and safe houses used by enslaved African Americans to flee to free states and Canada. Led by abolitionists and conductors, it provided a means for escaping slavery.
Civil Rights Act	This legislation was intended to put an end to segregation and discrimination based on race. It made discrimination in public places illegal and prohibited employment discrimination based on race, color, religion, sex, or national origin.
Voting Rights Act	This legislation was designed to address legal obstacles that hindered African Americans from voting. It banned discriminatory voting practices such as literacy tests and poll taxes, which were used to prevent Black voters from participating in elections.

GLOSSARY

FURTHER READING

Arthur Ashe

- "Days of Grace: A Memoir" by Arthur Ashe

- "Arthur Ashe: A Life" by Raymond Arsenault

Barack Obama

- "Dreams from My Father" by Barack Obama

- "The Audacity of Hope" by Barack Obama

Booker T. Washington

- "Up from Slavery" by Booker T. Washington

- "Booker T. Washington: Black Leadership in the Age of Jim Crow" by Raymond W. Smock

Carter G. Woodson

- "The Mis-Education of the Negro" by Carter G. Woodson

- "Carter G. Woodson: The Father of Black History" by Pat McKissack

Elizabeth Freeman

- "The Massachusetts Slave Who Won Her Freedom: The Story of Elizabeth Freeman" by Colleen Elizabeth Donohoe

Fannie Lou Hamer

- "This Little Light of Mine: The Life of Fannie Lou Hamer" by Kay Mills

- "Fannie Lou Hamer: The Life of a Civil Rights Icon" by Earnest N. Bracey

Frederick Douglass

- "Frederick Douglass: Prophet of Freedom" by David W. Blight

George Washington Carver

- "George Washington Carver: A Life" by Christina Vella

- "George Washington Carver: In His Own Words" by Gary R. Kremer

GLOSSARY

FURTHER READING

Harriet Tubman
- "Harriet Tubman: The Road to Freedom" by Catherine Clinton
- "Bound for the Promised Land: Harriet Tubman" by Kate Larson

Ida B. Wells
- "Crusade for Justice: The Autobiography of Ida B. Wells" by Ida B. Wells
- "Ida: A Sword Among Lions" by Paula J. Giddings

Jackie Robinson
- "Jackie Robinson: A Biography" by Arnold Rampersad
- "Jackie Robinson: An American Hero" by Sharon Robinson

John Lewis
- "Walking with the Wind: A Memoir of the Movement" by John Lewis
- "Across That Bridge: Life Lessons and a Vision for Change" by John Lewis

Langston Hughes
- "The Collected Poems of Langston Hughes"
- "The Weary Blues" by Langston Hughes

Madam C.J. Walker
- "On Her Own Ground: The Life and Times of Madam C. J. Walker" by A'Lelia Bundles
- "Madam C.J. Walker: Entrepreneur and Millionaire" by Noelle Henderson

Malcolm X
- "The Autobiography of Malcolm X" by Malcolm X and Alex Haley
- "Malcolm X: A Life of Reinvention" by Manning Marable

GLOSSARY

FURTHER READING

Marcus Garvey

- "Marcus Garvey: A Life" by Colin Grant

- "Marcus Garvey: Black Nationalist Leader" by Peggy Caravantes

Martin Luther King Jr.

- "Why We Can't Wait" by Martin Luther King Jr.

- "Letter from Birmingham Jail" by Martin Luther King Jr.

Maya Angelou

- "I Know Why the Caged Bird Sings" by Maya Angelou

- "The Heart of a Woman" by Maya Angelou

Medgar Evers

- "Medgar Evers: Mississippi Martyr" by Michael V. Williams

- "The Autobiography of Medgar Evers: A Hero's Life and Legacy Revealed Through His Writings, Letters, and Speeches" edited by Myrlie Evers-Williams

Muhammad Ali

- "The Greatest: My Own Story" by Muhammad Ali

- "Muhammad Ali: His Life and Times" by Thomas Hauser

Nelson Mandela

- "Long Walk to Freedom" by Nelson Mandela

- "Mandela: The Authorized Biography" by Anthony Sampson

Oprah Winfrey

- "Oprah: A Biography" by Kitty Kelley

- "The Path Made Clear: Discovering Your Life's Direction and Purpose" by Oprah Winfrey

GLOSSARY

FURTHER READING

Rosa Parks

- "The Rebellious Life of Mrs. Rosa Parks" by Jeanne Theoharis

- "Rosa Parks: My Story" by Rosa Parks

Ruby Bridges

- "Through My Eyes" by Ruby Bridges

- "The Story of Ruby Bridges" by Robert Coles

Shirley Chisholm

- "Unbought and Unbossed" by Shirley Chisholm

- "Shirley Chisholm: Catalyst for Change" by Barbara Winslow

Sojourner Truth

- "Narrative of Sojourner Truth" by Sojourner Truth

- "Sojourner Truth: A Life, A Symbol" by Nell Irvin Painter

Thurgood Marshall

- "Thurgood Marshall: American Revolutionary" by Juan Williams

- "Devil in the Grove: Thurgood Marshall, the Groveland Boys"

W.E.B. Du Bois

- "The Souls of Black Folk" by W.E.B. Du Bois

- "W.E.B. Du Bois: A Biography" by David Levering Lewis

Zora Neale Hurston

- "Their Eyes Were Watching God" by Zora Neale Hurston

- "Dust Tracks on a Road: An Autobiography" by Zora Neale Hurston

CHEEKYPRIMATE

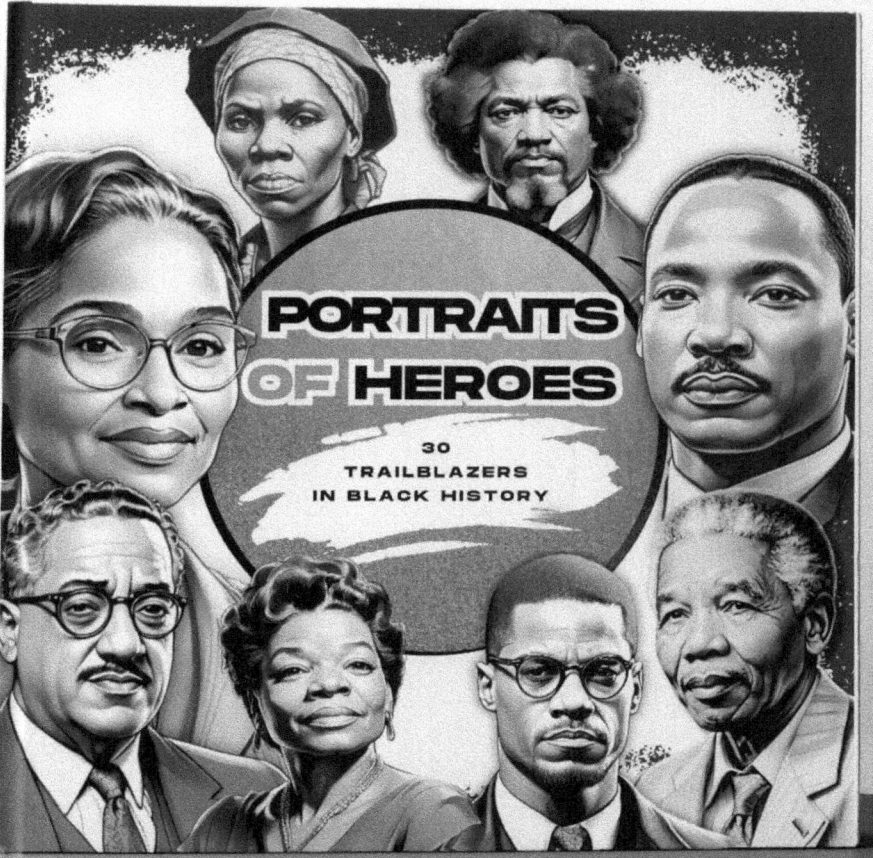

Share Your Thoughts!

We value your feedback and would appreciate it if you could share your thoughts in a review. Also, remember to scan the QR code to stay updated on the latest updates from Cheekyprimate!